# Picture reading

by W. MURRAY

with illustrations
by J. H. WINGFIELD

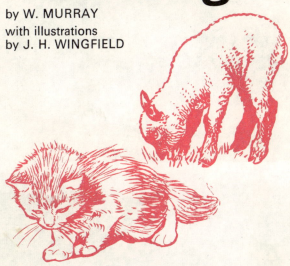

Publishers : Wills & Hepworth Ltd., Loughborough

First published 1972  Printed in England

Tell the story

*For those children who
are ready for reading –*

# The Ladybird Key
# Words Reading Scheme*

The full colour illustrations of the
Reading Scheme reflect the natural
interests and activities of happy
children, thus ensuring that every
child wants to read the books. Behind
the attractiveness of the scheme lies
a carefully planned scientific approach,
which results in rapid learning. There
is gradual introduction of new words
used, frequent repetition of these, and
a complete carry-over of vocabulary
from book to book.

*\* A descriptive booklet is available
from the Publishers.*

Peter

Jane

a dog     a tree     a ball

toys ———— a shop

# Peter        Jane

# a dog    a tree    a ball

# toys      a shop

First find a safe
place to cross.

Look all round for
traffic and listen.

If traffic is coming,
let it pass.
Look all round again.

When there is no traffic
near, walk straight
across the road.

# Crossing the road

# What do they mean?

# What do they do?

# What are they for?

2

# How many begin with the sound of t

10

How
many
begin
with the
sound of
**C**

# How many begin with the sound of
# b

Talk about this picture

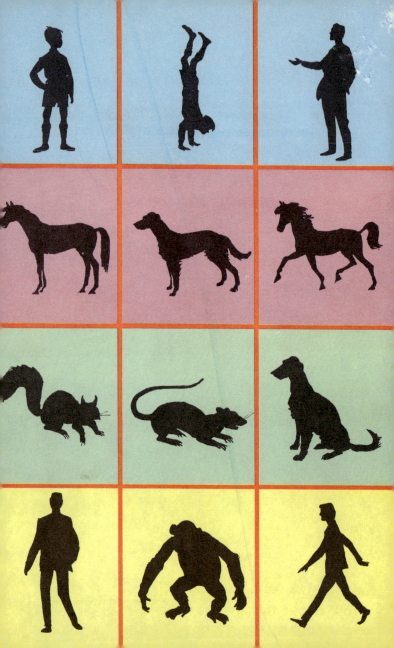

**LOOK**
and
find
another
like this

and this

and this

and this

**LOOK**
and
find
another
like this

and this

and this

and this

# LOOK and find
## another like this

and this

and this

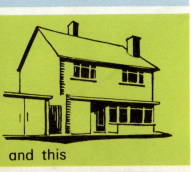 

and this

# LOOK and find
another like this

and this

and this

and this

# Look and find her baby

and hers

and hers

and hers

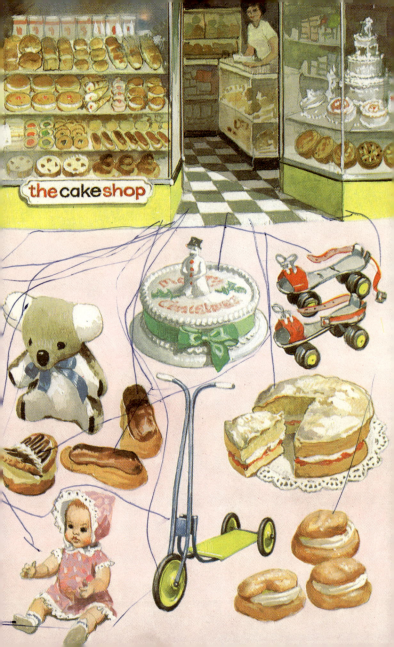

the cakeshop

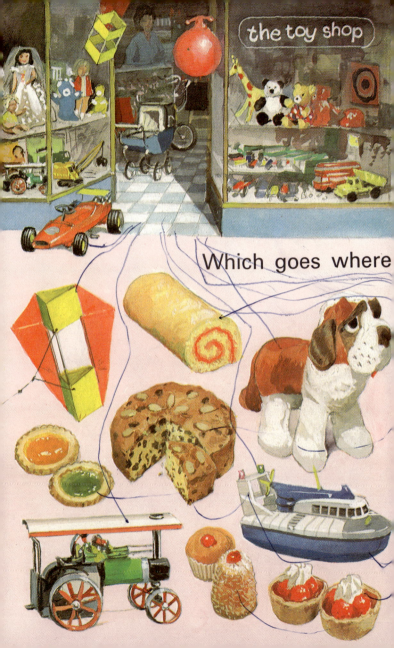

the toy shop

Which goes where

# Which go together?

# Learning colours

# Learning colours

# Learning colours

**2**

Plant your
bulbs now

Tulips
Daffodils
Hyacinth

tulips

**4**

**6**

**Tell the story**

**Tell the story**

1

3

5

Talk about this picture